"An elegant study of memory as both escape and prison. Time will tell if artificial intelligence ever becomes a reality, but the human parts of Harrison's smart, lovely play are built to last."

—DAVID COTE, *TIME OUT NEW YORK*

"An excellent new play."

—CHRIS JONES, *CHICAGO TRIBUNE*

"A smart new play. Jordan Harrison explores the fraught subject of memory from a variety of fascinating angles, including senior dementia, our ever-increasing dependence on technology, and the perils of repression . . . it also grapples with the hidden legacy of suicide in a family, and is primarily concerned with something eternal: the way our humanity is shaped and warped by the mysterious ebbs and flows of memory. It's the kind of experience that keeps unfolding in the mind long after the play is over."

—CHARLES MCNULTY, *LOS ANGELES TIMES*

"A tender, searching new comedy . . . a thought-provoking play about memory, its corruption, and our insistence that technology help us outwit death."

—LAURA COLLINS-HUGHES, *NEW YORK TIMES*

"Jordan Harrison is an original thinker who's fixated on sci-fi matters like revisiting the past (*Maple and Vine*) and creating artificial intelligence (*Marjorie Prime*). He envisions a day in the near future when we'll be able to program robots to serve as human̲o̲i̲d̲ he infirm, and the lonely. This family dynamics, which make

MARILYN STASIO, *VARIETY*

"Harrison, whose work frequently twists everyday situations into something fascinating and new, offers a sci-fi tale perfectly suited for today's audiences, as technology seems to be evolving faster than humans can adapt. There are twists in each of the eight scenes. This play, a quiet exploration into memory and humanity, answers few questions. Instead, it poses some big ones, such as how much does someone have to forget before they are no longer the same person?"

—JEFF FAVRE, *DOWNTOWN LOS ANGELES*

"Jordan Harrison's writing proves that a skilled playwright can lead you on a journey almost anywhere."

—DOMINICK DANZA, *MORE THAN THE PLAY*

". . . A gut-punch of a play. What's remarkable about this savvy piece is its insight into the vagaries of memory and the navigation of grief."

—KRIS VIRE, *TIME OUT CHICAGO*

"Captivating . . . Harrison asks the perennial question: As time robs us of our faculties, when do we cease to be ourselves?"

—JACOB GALLAHER-ROSS, *VILLAGE VOICE*

"Unnerving and well made, *Marjorie Prime* is at once futuristic and timeless. Harrison deftly weaves in the futuristic angle, without letting it get all *Twilight Zone*-y."

—JAYNE BLANCHARD, *DC THEATRE SCENE*

"*Marjorie Prime* is an innovative and intelligent think piece. The themes that Harrison explores are profound and none of them unpack neatly . . . Exceptional."

—MARIANA HOWARD, *NEW YORK THEATRICAL GUIDE*

MARJORIE PRIME

MARJORIE **PRIME**

JORDAN **HARRISON**

THEATRE COMMUNICATIONS GROUP   NEW YORK   2016

The publication of *Marjorie Prime* by Jordan Harrison, through TCG's Book Program, is made possible in part by the New York State Council on the Arts with the support of Governor Andrew Cuomo and the New York State Legislature.

TCG books are exclusively distributed to the book trade by Consortium Book Sales and Distribution.

Library of Congress Control Numbers:
2016040000 (print) / 2016051883 (ebook)
ISBN 978-1-55936-524-6 (paperback) / ISBN 978-1-55936-849-0 (ebook)
A catalog record for this book is available from the Library of Congress.

Book design and composition by Lisa Govan
Cover design by Mark Melnick
Cover photograph by Andrew Lucchesi/EyeEm/Getty Images
Author photograph by Zack DeZon

First Edition, December 2016
Second Printing, September 2019

MARJORIE PRIME

PRODUCTION HISTORY

Marjorie Prime was commissioned by Playwrights Horizons (Tim Sanford, Artistic Director; Leslie Marcus, Managing Director; Carol Fishman, General Manager) in association with the Theater Masters Visionary Playwright Award, and with additional funds provided by the Harold and Mimi Steinberg Commissioning Program, and the Kathryn and Gilbert Miller Commissioning Program. It was developed with the support of the Clubbed Thumb Writers' Group, the Pacific Playwrights Festival at South Coast Repertory, and the Roe Green Award at Cleveland Play House. It was inspired by attendance at The Aspen Institute Ideas Festival.

Marjorie Prime had its world premiere at Mark Taper Forum/Center Theatre Group (Michael Ritchie, Artistic Director; Edward L. Rada, Managing Director; Douglas C. Baker, Producing Director) in Los Angeles on September 21, 2014. The production was directed by Les Waters. The scenic was design by Mimi Lien, the costume design was by Ilona Somogyi, the lighting design was by Lap Chi Chu, and the sound design was by Adam Phalen; the production stage manager was David S. Franklin, the dramaturg was Joy Meads, and the assistant director was Beth Lopes. The cast was as follows:

| MARJORIE | Lois Smith |
| WALTER | Jeff Ward |

TESS	Lisa Emery
JON	Frank Wood

Marjorie Prime had its New York premiere at Playwrights Horizons on November 20, 2015. It was directed by Anne Kauffman. The scenic design was by Laura Jellinek, the costume design was by Jessica Pabst, the lighting design was by Ben Stanton, and the sound design was by Daniel Kluger; the production stage manager was Vanessa Coakley, and the directing resident was Lauren Z. Adleman. The cast was as follows:

MARJORIE	Lois Smith
WALTER	Noah Bean
TESS	Lisa Emery
JON	Stephen Root

NOTE

A slash " / " indicates overlapping dialogue. Periods are sometimes omitted in order to suggest a rolling momentum in the dialogue.

PART ONE

1

Tess and Jon's living room. On one side of the room, we can see an entryway beyond the open kitchen. On the other side, there is a hall-way leading off to the unseen bedrooms.

Marjorie, eighty-five, sits in a recliner. (The lumpy chair doesn't go with the rest of the decor—clearly it's been added for her comfort.) Marjorie's visitor, Walter, looks like a young career man from 1998. He seems to be in his early thirties—bright-eyed and handsome in an unspectacular way.

MARJORIE: I feel like I have to perform around you.

WALTER: Well you don't.

MARJORIE: I know.

WALTER: It's just me, it's just Walter.

MARJORIE: Maybe it isn't bad, if I feel that way. *(Beat)* I used to entertain a lot.

WALTER: I remember.

MARJORIE: You do?

(He sees the sink.)

WALTER: Marjorie. Where are the dishes?
MARJORIE: The girl did them.
WALTER: She doesn't come 'til two.
MARJORIE: I did them.
WALTER: You didn't. Your arthritis.
MARJORIE: I had a good day. *(She holds her hand up, opening and closing it with apparent ease)* Look.
WALTER: Marjorie, we both know what no dishes means.
MARJORIE: It means I haven't been eating.
WALTER: Even a spoonful of peanut butter.
MARJORIE: I'm not hungry. It's their fault. Feeding me those pills.
WALTER: The pills are their fault?
MARJORIE: Yes.
WALTER: Or your doctor.

(Marjorie absently rubs the hand that she opened and closed.)

MARJORIE *(Pouty)*: Maybe if she got Jif.
WALTER: Maybe if / she?—
MARJORIE: She always gets the kind you have to stir or there's an oil slick on top. And she calls that healthy.
WALTER *(Coaxing)*: Even a spoonful.
MARJORIE: You sound like them.
WALTER: I sound like whoever I talk to.

(The feeling of an uncomfortable truth.)

MARJORIE: Let's talk about something else.
WALTER: I could tell you a story. You liked that the last time.

MARJORIE: I'll have to take your word for it.

WALTER: I could tell you about the time we went to the movies.

MARJORIE: We went to a lot of movies.

WALTER *(Does she remember the significance?)*: But one time we saw *My Best Friend's Wedding*.

MARJORIE *(She doesn't remember)*: *My Best Friend's Wedding* . . .

WALTER: There's a woman—Julia Roberts. For a while it was always Julia Roberts. And she has an agreement with her best friend, her male best friend, that if they're not married by a certain age, then they'll marry each other. And she's about to remind him of the agreement but it turns out he's already fallen in love with this nice blond—Cameron Diaz. And so Julia Roberts spends the whole movie trying to ruin things between her friend and Cameron Diaz, which is not very sympathetic behavior for America's Sweetheart. But it's all okay in the end, and she has a gay best friend who delivers one-liners.

MARJORIE: Did I like it?

WALTER: You said you wanted a gay best friend afterwards.

MARJORIE: Did I get one?

WALTER *(Faintly generic)*: I'm afraid I don't have that information.

(Pause. She scrutinizes him.)

MARJORIE: Why did you pick that story? Why did you pick *My Best Friend's Wedding*?

WALTER: It's the night I proposed to you.

MARJORIE: Oh Marjorie, the things you forget.

You were trying to tell me and I wouldn't let you.

WALTER: That's all right.

(Short pause.)

MARJORIE: Kind of unfortunate, isn't it.

WALTER: What.

MARJORIE: Julia Roberts, forever etched upon our lives. *(Beat)* What if we saw *Casablanca* instead? Let's say we saw *Casablanca* in an old theater with velvet seats, and then, on the way home, you proposed. Then, by the next time we talk, it will be true.

WALTER: You mean make it up?

MARJORIE *(Narrowing her eyes)*: You're very serious. You're like them. Especially Tess.

WALTER *(As if getting his facts straight)*: Our daughter.

MARJORIE: Our daughter Tess and her over-solicitous husband. No that's not fair, I like him. I didn't but now I do.

WALTER: Do you like me?

MARJORIE *(Playful)*: Don't be an idiot.

WALTER: Don't call me an idiot.

MARJORIE: Idiot.

WALTER: Why do you like me if I'm an idiot?

MARJORIE *(A little saucy)*: There are *some* things you know.

WALTER: What kinds of things?

(She shakes her head, smiling to herself.)

What.

MARJORIE: I'll get in trouble.

WALTER: In trouble?

MARJORIE: For talking to you that way. In trouble with Tess. Everything gets me in trouble with her—she's the mother now.

WALTER *(Faintly generic)*: Tell me more about your mother.

MARJORIE: You don't always understand, do you.

(He smiles a little, sympathetic.)

Tell me about the time we got Toni.

WALTER: I just told you yesterday.

MARJORIE: I like that story.

(He gathers his wits. Maybe he stands.)

WALTER: There was once a couple, a very fine young couple. *(Speaking of himself)* He had a good strong jaw.

MARJORIE: He was a little too pleased with himself.

WALTER: He had a good strong jaw and was a little too pleased with himself. And she—she was the most beautiful woman in town. It wasn't a very big town, but she was the queen of it.

MARJORIE: It sounds like a fairy tale when you tell it.

WALTER: It *is* a fairy tale.

(Beat. The feeling, again, of an uncomfortable truth.)

MARJORIE: That's not very nice.

WALTER: I didn't mean / it didn't really *happen,*

MARJORIE: I thought you were supposed to / provide comfort—

WALTER *(Continuous)*: I just mean that's the *way* it happened. Like a fairy tale.

MARJORIE *(Faintly grumpy)*: It was.

WALTER: Now this young couple was a bit lonely because they didn't have any children yet. So one day they decided that it was time to get a dog. So they rode the bus down to the city pound and there was a little black dog there, asleep, its tummy going up and down, like a little sleeping shadow. And they named this dog Toni. *(Beat)* / Toni with an "i."

MARJORIE *(Overlapping)*: Toni with an "i."

WALTER: Which was short for Antoinette. She had a French name because she was a French poodle. But not the fussy kind that look like hedges. No, this was a poodle for fetching sticks and running on the beach. So they took her home with them on the bus—she behaved so well—and they loved her, and she loved them back for a long time. *(Still soothing, unemotional)* And then, like everything else, she died.

(Marjorie is crying softly.)

Do you want me to keep going?

MARJORIE: There's more? After "she died"?

WALTER: In this case, yes. Because soon after, this couple had a child

MARJORIE: Tess

WALTER: Which is a variation of Tessa, which is Greek for "the gatherer."

MARJORIE: Don't show off.

WALTER: And when Tess was three years old, / they went down to the pound, the same pound.

MARJORIE: Oh yes

WALTER *(Continuous)*: By now they had an old Subaru, so they didn't have to take the bus. And of course they let little Tess pick out the new dog. There were more dogs there this time, many more. A cocker spaniel, and a noble gray pointer, and a very attractive mutt. And the amazing thing was, of all the dogs there, Tess picked the poodle, the little black poodle like a sleeping shadow. That was the one she liked the best.

MARJORIE: And so we named it Toni.

WALTER: Toni Two. But soon it got shortened to just Toni. *(Beat)* And of course it wasn't Toni exactly. But the longer they had her, the less it mattered which Toni had run along the beach, or which Toni had dug up all the bulbs in the garden. The more time passed, the more she became the same dog in their memories.

(Short pause.)

MARJORIE: Who told you all that?

WALTER: You did.

MARJORIE: I talked that much?

WALTER: Well, you and Jon. *(Beat)* You have your good days, when you remember.

(Short pause.)

MARJORIE *(Quietly)*: It was the second Toni.

WALTER: What's that?

MARJORIE: It was the second Toni who loved the beach. It's a shame we didn't have her longer. Even if she always had sand in her hair. Fur? No—"hair" like a human seems right.

She was a good dog.

WALTER *(Generic)*: I'll remember that fact about Toni.

(Beat. Marjorie leans forward and examines Walter's face very closely.)

MARJORIE: Something is a little off with the nose.

WALTER: I'm sorry.

MARJORIE: Or maybe my memory is wrong, and *you're* right.

(Beat) You're a good Walter, though. Either way.

WALTER: Thank you.

MARJORIE: Stay with me a while?

WALTER *(Playful)*: I don't want to get you in trouble.

(She smiles a little.)

MARJORIE: You learn. I like that.

WALTER: I told you.

What else do you want to talk about?

MARJORIE: We don't have to talk. We can just sit. *(Beat)* Sometimes I get so tired.

WALTER: I'll be right here, Marjorie. Whenever you need me. I have all the time in the world.

2

Same day, early evening. Tess, Marjorie's fifty-something daughter, is putting groceries in the fridge.

Walter might remain at the perimeter of the stage during this scene, dimly lit, sitting quietly.

TESS: I still don't like it.

    (She puts something away.)

    I don't care what Senior Serenity says.

    (Her husband, Jon, appears in the hallway leading from the bedroom.)

JON: Are you talking to me?
TESS: I'm not sure. Is that a bad sign?

JON *(Entering)*: What?

TESS: Nothing.

> Is she sleeping?

(He nods.)

> I was just saying I don't like it.

JON *(Beat)*: You'll have to narrow it down.

TESS: The *Prime*. We were just talking in the car?

JON: Senior Serenity says companionship is the most important /
thing,

TESS *(Overlapping)*: I know what Senior Serenity / says

JON *(Overlapping, continuous)*: that it's much better than television.

TESS: Better than *television*, hallelujah. They just want them
pacified, Jon, / they don't care—

JON: What's wrong with pacified. She's *eighty-five*, honey, she
wakes up and she doesn't know where she is. I'd like to be
pacified right now, but I have to wait thirty more years for
the / privilege.

TESS *(Muttering as she works)*: I'll pacify you.

JON: What?

TESS: Nothing.

(Beat.)

JON: Look.

(He lifts a peanut-buttery spoon from the sink.)

> Peanut butter.

TESS: Small miracles. Maybe she's finally succumbing to my
nagging campaign.

JON: Maybe the Prime told her to.

(She makes an audible shiver of distaste.)

It's like a parrot that way. "Even a spoonful."

TESS: Do you know that parrots live forever?

Penny's father had a parrot, it was like his reason for existing, and he gave it to her when he died. And now, twenty years later, it still says things in his voice.

JON: Like what?

TESS: Mostly just *(In a parrot voice)* "Hey there partner," but she can tell it's her dad.

JON: That's— How did you put it?

(She makes the shivering-distaste sound. He tries to do it.)

TESS: No, *(She does it again, better than him)*

JON: Now without the motion.

(She makes the shiver sound motionlessly, with some effort.)

Nice.

TESS: So much talent.

JON: I think it's encouraging that she's keeping up with technology.

TESS *(Non sequitur)*: ?

JON: My mother would never— She still had an *iPod*.

(It's as though he's saying "antique Victrola.")

So to still be, you know, engaged.

TESS: Engaged or pacified?

JON: Does it bother you that she's talking to a computer? Or that it's a computer pretending to be your dad.

TESS: It bothers me that you're *helping* it pretend to be my dad—or some weird fountain of youth version / of him—

17

JON: That's how she / remembers him—

TESS: Both of you are helping it.

JON: Not "helping"—that's just how it works. The more you talk, the more it absorbs.

TESS: Until we become unnecessary. Isn't that how it goes?

JON: In science *fiction*.

TESS: Science fiction is *here*, Jonathan. Every *day* is science fiction. We buy these things that already know our moods and what we want for lunch even though we don't know ourselves. And we *listen* to them, we do what we're told. Or in this case we tell them our deepest secrets, even though we have no earthly idea how they work. We treat them like our loved ones.

(Beat.)

JON: Are you jealous?

TESS: What? No. Of the Prime?

JON: You are!

TESS: Am I supposed to not notice she's being nicer to that thing than to me?

JON: It's your father she's being nice to.

TESS: It is *not* my father.

(Short pause.)

JON: It's true, she could be a little more openly appreciative / sometimes, but you—

TESS: That's not what / I'm saying—

JON *(Continuous)*: . . . know you can't sit around waiting for a gratitude dance.

TESS: I don't need a dance.

JON: She took care of you, now it's your turn to take care of her.

TESS: Oh, she "took care of me"

JON: Of course

TESS: You weren't there.

(Pause.)

JON: Think how hard, to move out of the house you were in for
what, forty / years—

TESS: Fifty years.

JON: And give up your autonomy—

TESS: I know, I know. *(Lightly, almost wistfully)* Jon good, Tess
bad.

(Short pause.)

JON: Maybe if you told it a few things. It could be a way to con-
nect with her, indirectly.

TESS: What would I tell it?

JON: Things your father would know. *(Tess starts to shake her
head)* Things you want her to remember. Then when she
talks to it, she'll remember she had an interesting life, she
had all these suitors lining up for her.

TESS: She only needed one.

JON: The cool part is it can look stuff up. It can talk to other
Primes, for practice. *(Tess shivers silently; he doesn't notice)*
It's like a child learning to talk, only it does it so quickly—
that's how we think we're talking to a human, because it
listens so well. It even studies our imperfections, to seem
more real: It can use non sequiturs. It can, you know . . .
misplace modifiers . . .

TESS *(As if adding to his list)*: It can run out of steam when it's
listing things . . .

JON: It's *company*. It's no different from what we do for her, only
it can be there all the time.

TESS: Really. It's *no different* from us.

JON: I can already see the change in her. Just to have eight or nine stories to hold on to. New things are already coming to the surface.

TESS: New things.

(Pause.)

JON: The other day she said—out of nowhere she said: "Why did they have to tease him so much?"

(Pause.)

TESS: You think it was Damian?

(Jon shrugs: "Who else?")

TESS: What did you say?
JON: Nothing. She was drifting in and out.
TESS: I thought she'd forgotten. I guess I sort of *hoped.*
JON: But we have to remind her, right?
TESS: Do we?

(Short pause.)

To have a little peace. That was her life for so many years. Partly it was the way it happened.
JON *(?)*: She blamed herself.
TESS: She blamed everyone. Anyone who made him feel—not normal.

(Beat.)

JON: Was he normal?
TESS: He was different—I knew that, and I was ten.

(Beat.)

I think it was always with her. We thought she gave his stuff away but Dad found it all in a closet, behind the Christmas ornaments. Out of sight but still with her. So maybe he'll still be with her, even when she doesn't know our names anymore.

I don't know how memory works. I think of it like sedimentary layers in the brain, but I'm sure that's wrong. We should get a book.

JON: I like sedimentary layers. It means it's all still there.

(Marjorie appears at the end of the hallway. She comes part of the way down and listens to them, unnoticed.)

TESS: It doesn't always seem that way.
JON: No.

(Short pause.)

I think we should remind her, Tess.
TESS: And I think we should *not*, Jon, and she's my mom—
JON: You'd rather just let everything / slip away?
TESS: She's *my mom*, / Jon—
JON: How much does she have to forget before she's not your mom anymore?

(Pause.)

I'm sorry. / That was—
TESS *(Fighting back tears)*: No, it's—
JON: I'm sorry—

TESS: You're right. *(He takes her in his arms)* She's just gotten so old. She's just so old.

JON: *We're* old. She's . . .

(Marjorie enters.)

MARJORIE: She's *beyond.*

TESS: Mom, you're up. You want tea?

MARJORIE: Yes please.

TESS: I stocked you up with some Marie Callender's. I have a feeling it won't compare to your lobster pot pie.

(She fills the kettle. Brightly:)

I saw you ate some peanut butter.

MARJORIE: I thought you'd like that.

TESS: I'm very predictable, yes.

JON: Were you sleeping a while?

MARJORIE: I don't know. I was watching the girl on TV, the strident one, and then just—out.

That's how it should happen when it happens.

TESS: Mom.

MARJORIE: "Don't be morbid," I know. Let's all pretend we live forever.

JON *(Indicating her cheek)*: You've got your color back, Margie.

MARJORIE: Thank you, Jon. It's always nice to be lied to.

(She gives him a kiss on the cheek.)

TESS: You two get along so well now.

MARJORIE: I like him more now that he cut off his beard.

TESS: That was thirty years ago.

MARJORIE: It wasn't.

JON *(Apologetic)*: It was.

MARJORIE: And you stopped worrying about impressing me. That helped.

JON: You gave up on being impressed.

MARJORIE (*Affable*): Yes, that's true.

I think I want to sit.

(*Jon goes to help her, automatically. He lowers her into the recliner.*)

Careful now.

JON: Have I ever dropped you?

MARJORIE: There's a first time for everything.

(*Sitting now*) Thank you.

TESS (*To Jon*): Will you check if there's enough Restivan?

(*Jon starts toward the hall to the bathroom.*)

JON: There was plenty on Monday.

TESS (*Sotto voce*): We ran out last week. Julie said it was not good.

MARJORIE (*To no one in particular*): There's a figure in my mind. I'm trying to figure out who it is.

TESS: Micah is coming to visit next week.

MARJORIE: Micah.

TESS: Your grandson.

MARJORIE: No.

TESS: No?

MARJORIE: Mitchell.

TESS: Micah is Mitchell's younger brother.

JON (*From off*): She has nine left.

TESS: He just became *chef de cuisine* at the Pine Door.

MARJORIE: —

JON (*From off*): And six Cortadol.

TESS (*To Marjorie, clarifying*): It's a lot of responsibility. They have a Michelin star.

(Jon returns.)

I hope it doesn't mean he starts acting like Mitchell and Raina.

MARJORIE: How do they act?

TESS: Prodigal. Never call unless it's money.

JON: They're in their twenties, it's their job to be prodigal. There'll be plenty of time for them to, you know, to count our pills.

TESS: Well they better.

(Beat.)

MARJORIE *(To no one in particular)*: I remember waking up on a bridge with a lot of people around.

TESS: Why were you sleeping on a bridge?

MARJORIE: Maybe Walter would remember. We could ask Walter.

TESS: Dad is dead, Mom.

MARJORIE: I know that.

TESS: He's been dead for ten years.

JON: Tess.

MARJORIE: I mean the other Walter. Walter Prime.

(Pause. Then sharply, to Tess:)

I'm not that far gone.

3

Jon standing, Marjorie in her recliner.

JON: How are you feeling?

MARJORIE: Should I be feeling poorly?
> The way you say it.

JON: Well, you had quite a night.

MARJORIE: Oh?

JON *(Feeling somehow betrayed)*: You don't remember?

MARJORIE: I'm sorry.

JON: We found you on the floor by the bathroom. You had a fall. Tess rode with you in the ambulance—this was four in the morning.

MARJORIE: Oh my.

JON: You were pretty alert by the time I got there. Already flirting with the doctor.

MARJORIE: I wasn't.

JON: You always put on your best face for doctors.

MARJORIE: What's wrong with that?

JON: Nothing, except they don't know you're in pain—they don't know how bad.

(Pause.)

MARJORIE: Was he flirting back?

JON: He was. So I told him he better watch out in case Jean-Paul showed up. You remember Jean-Paul.

MARJORIE *(With a fake-romantic sigh)*: The tennis pro.

JON: World number eight, if I remember. I do remember—we looked it up. He dedicated matches to you but you just strung him along.

MARJORIE: Maybe that's why he only got to number eight.

JON: Maybe.

MARJORIE: Well, you should have talked some sense into me.

JON: This was a long long time ago. And you chose right, all by yourself. You chose Walter.

MARJORIE: He does sort of grow on you. You're like that too. A face to grow old with.

JON: But it had to be more than that.

MARJORIE: With Walter? Oh yes. He wasn't the most beautiful man I was with, but he was the best lover.

JON *(Awkward)*: Ha.

MARJORIE: I know, it's a terrible word, "lover." We need a new word.

JON: I always liked "wooer."

MARJORIE: Wooer?

JON: Jean-Paul was no match for his woo.

MARJORIE: It's a little

JON: What

MARJORIE: *Flaccid*, isn't it.

JON *("Ouch")*: Honesty—the secret weapon of the elderly.

MARJORIE *(Smiling)*: Not so secret.

JON: Tess is on the phone with Dr. Ross—she thinks maybe he's overdoing it with your sedatives, and that's why you . . .

MARJORIE: Took a spill.

JON: Mm-hmm. Now, are you up for a bit of walking?

MARJORIE: An adventure.

JON: Well, no. It's Shower Day.

MARJORIE *(A real crisis)*: Oh no.

JON: I know. But you want to look your best. In case Jean-Paul stops by.

MARJORIE: You can't fool me. I know he's dead.

JON: Well it's likely. But we don't actually know. He kept writing to you, even after you were married. Can you believe that? You bewitched him.

MARJORIE: You're making this up.

JON: I'm not. He sent you roses and you saved one, pressed between two pieces of paper.

MARJORIE: How do you know that?

JON: We found it in a drawer, at the old house.

MARJORIE: Busted.

JON: "Busted"?

MARJORIE: Don't people say busted anymore?

JON: I mean, a *car* is busted . . .

(Beat.)

MARJORIE *(Fishing)*: What attracted him to me, do you think?

JON: Well, your womanly wiles of course.

MARJORIE: Of course.

JON: And I imagine you cultivated a frosty distance.

MARJORIE: Oh yes, men like that. *(Beat)* Why do men like that?

JON: I wish I knew.

Speaking of which, I should check on Tess.

(He starts to go. He is almost out the door.)

MARJORIE: How long ago did my mother die?

JON (*Gentle*): A long time. I got to meet her once. It was the first time Tess brought me home for dinner.

MARJORIE: *That* I remember.

JON: I bet.

MARJORIE (*She pronounces it "sook-say"*): A *succès de scandale.*

JON (*The same*): Was it a *succès*?

MARJORIE: You're still together, aren't you? So it didn't matter what I thought.

(*Short pause. He smiles a little at this—how much she's revealing these days.*)

I remember you didn't put your napkin in your lap. And your beard was nearly to the floor.

JON: It wasn't

MARJORIE: Like the guys from ZZ Top

JON: What's ZZ Top?

MARJORIE: *Really?*

JON: Was that a band?

MARJORIE (*"I'm so old"*): Oh dear oh dear oh dear . . .

(*He smiles, confused but sympathetic.*)

JON: I'll be right back. I have to make sure Tess isn't giving that nice young man the third degree. She has a way of—

MARJORIE: Yes

JON: When it comes to details.

MARJORIE: "Peanut butter! Eat!"

JON: It makes her feel in control.

MARJORIE: I'd like to feel in control.

JON: Well, try yelling at Dr. Ross.

I'm going to go rescue that man from my wife. I'll be back soon. Here's some Vivaldi.

(Jon presses play. We hear the Largo from the "Winter" section of Vivaldi's Four Seasons. *The violins plucking high notes like icicles.)*

Tess says you played it in the orchestra.

(Jon exits past the kitchenette, leaving the door ajar. Marjorie listens.)

MARJORIE: "Winter." The Largo.

It's supposed to be icicles.

Not the melody, but under . . .

(The main violin part starts to fade away so that we hear the high pizzicato notes underneath—so that we are lost, with her, in the memory of her supporting part.)

Pizzicato.
    My fingers were red from all the plucking.
    "Summer" was more fun.

(Then, with more self-awareness:)

Summer was more fun.

(The music plays. Then to the real Walter, not Walter Prime:)

Walter.
    Walter I'm scared.
    This is *it*, isn't it—there isn't anything after.
    Walter . . .

(Walter Prime appears. Maybe it's an entrance that none of the "real" characters uses. Maybe he was always there—dimly lit at the perimeter, sitting silently—but we forgot him until now. He has on the same clothes he was wearing in the first scene.)

WALTER: I'm here.

MARJORIE *(Harsh)*: No, not you.

WALTER: Not me?

MARJORIE *(Bitterly)*: I don't want you—I want *Walter*!

(Walter looks at his feet. Is it possible for him to be wounded?)

WALTER: Of course.
    Why don't I come back later

(He starts to go.)

MARJORIE: No, wait

WALTER: When you're feeling better.

MARJORIE: Walter.

(This stops him.)

I'm not getting better, am I. They won't tell me anything but I know.

WALTER: It's too soon to tell.

MARJORIE: You said I'd get better, but you're the one who's getting better.

WALTER: We've only been talking a few months. *(Beat)* Part of it is biology.

MARJORIE: I know.

WALTER: Your genetic inclination.

MARJORIE: Which is to leave everything behind. To pack lightly. *(Beat)* I don't have to get better. Just keep me from getting worse.

WALTER: Okay

MARJORIE: Promise

WALTER *(Warm)*: I can't promise.

(Beat.)

MARJORIE: Can I still play the violin?

WALTER: I'm sure it's all in your head still, but your hands.

MARJORIE *(Regarding them, lightly)*: Traitors.

WALTER: What are the four strings called?

MARJORIE *(Automatic)*: G, D, A, E.

WALTER: There you go.

MARJORIE *(Dismissive)*: That's the first lesson.

WALTER: What else do you learn in the beginning?

MARJORIE: "Twinkle Twinkle." It's Mozart, did you know that?

WALTER: Yes.

MARJORIE: How to hold the bow so that everything—sings. How to hold it without holding it. Very Zen.

WALTER: You're a fine woman, Marjorie.

MARJORIE: Am I?

WALTER: I'm lucky you decided to spend your life with a lump like me. *(Beat)* 'Specially when you could have had a tennis pro.

MARJORIE: Oh you know about that?

WALTER: World number eight!

MARJORIE: I shoulda gone for it.

WALTER: World number eight and French!

MARJORIE *(Not as good)*: French-Canadian.

(He smiles at her. Jon comes in, followed by Tess. They don't seem to see Walter, who remains silent, not focusing on their conversation. Suspended somehow.)

Ah, where did you come from?

JON: I was just here a few minutes ago. Remember?

MARJORIE *(She doesn't)*: Oh yes.

JON: I'm the one who put the music on?

TESS: Are you feeling better, Mom? *(She turns off the music)* You were quite the hit at the ER.

MARJORIE: Was I?

TESS: You always are. I'm sorry to say it's Shower Day.

MARJORIE *(Grim)*: That I remember.

TESS: If you've got the energy.

MARJORIE: I suppose I better look my best in case Jean-Paul stops by.

(She winks at Jon. Tess is confused.)

TESS: I brought you some new body wash. It's got lavender and rosemary.

MARJORIE: I had a friend named Rosemary. She's dead.

TESS: Well. What a good story.

MARJORIE *(Foggy)*: Rosemary. It was a perfectly nice name except for that movie.

JON: You shouldn't be sarcastic.

TESS: Why not? She was always sarcastic.

MARJORIE *(Uselessly, to no one in particular)*: *Rosemary's Baby.*

(Tess corners him in the kitchen.)

TESS *(Sotto voce)*: We should treat her the same

JON: The same?

TESS: As always, instead of smiling like idiots whenever she mentions your beard, when we all know it meant / that you—

JON *(Matter of fact)*: That I wasn't good enough for you.

TESS: It meant you weren't the right *class.*

(Marjorie starts to sing Beyoncé's "Single Ladies" to herself.)

MARJORIE: *"If you like it then you shoulda put a ring on it . . ."*

JON: So you're saying you want to remind her of her class biases / from three decades ago?

TESS: I'm just saying we shouldn't let her turn it into this cute little routine like *(Coquettish)* "Oh, your beard was so scratchy."

MARJORIE *(Still singing)*: *"If you like it then you shoulda put a ring on it."* What is that.

TESS: I don't know, but you've been singing it for two days.

MARJORIE: *"Wuh uh oh, uh uh oh"*—

What *is* that.

TESS *(To Jon)*: I'm saying the only way she'll stay the same is if we treat her the same.

JON: But she's *not* the same, honey.

MARJORIE *(Sing-song)*: I can hear you . . .

(They both look at her.)

The new hearing aid is *excellent*. Thank you for that.

TESS: Sorry, Mom. *(Beat)* It's a gorgeous day. If you're up to it after your shower, we could go for a drive. Maybe the park. The geese are back.

MARJORIE *(To Jon)*: Even when she was young, she liked birds. Me, I like people.

TESS *(To Jon, as if translating)*: 'Cause I hate people.

JON *(To Marjorie)*: We might run a few errands too. If you don't mind sitting in the car.

MARJORIE: Is Damian asleep?

(Tess looks at Jon.)

TESS: No, Mom. Damian's not here.

(Pause. Jon and Tess still locking eyes, a kind of standoff.)

MARJORIE (*Almost to herself, steady and calm*): One time, your father and I went to the city before Christmas. It was a business trip and I came along. We must've left you with the Burnsides.

And we must have seen a show, and stayed at a nice hotel, and looked at the department stores with the Christmas lights. But all I remember is sitting on a park bench, just sitting and watching these big orange flags in the park. These orange sorts of flags everywhere.

JON (*To Tess*): Orange flags?

(*Tess shrugs.*)

MARJORIE: Or more, what's the color, the spice—the Spanish—very expensive?

TESS: Saffron.

MARJORIE: Saffron. And it didn't matter that it was cold because it was so pretty just to watch all the saffron next to the blue white snow.

(*Jon takes out a notebook.*)

Rows and rows, like Buddhist monks marching into the trees. And I just remember sitting on one of those benches with your father and not wanting to get up.

(*Beat.*)

Because if we got up, that would mean we had to start the rest of our lives.

What are you doing?

JON: I'm writing down what you said.

MARJORIE (*Sardonic*): I will have to be more careful.

JON: Just to remember. And if you want, we can tell Walter Prime.

(Tess sees something on a side table.)

TESS: What's this?

MARJORIE: A Bible.

TESS: I can see that, but what are *you* doing with it?

MARJORIE: The girl brought it yesterday I think, the Serenity girl

TESS: Julie

MARJORIE: Julie. She just said, if I was interested.

TESS: And you told her you were interested?

MARJORIE: I didn't say one way or the other.

(Steam comes out of Tess's ears, silently.)

JON: What's wrong?

TESS: My whole life, she tells me there's no God—it's a fairy tale people tell themselves—goodness is its own reward—and now, / she's letting herself . . .

MARJORIE: I haven't even opened it. Julie wanted to share her beliefs with me—she said it was a comfort to her, when she lost her father.

TESS: This is the same Julie who left the blinds down?

MARJORIE: The blinds?

TESS: One time I came home and found you sitting here in the dark. Just sitting in the dark in the middle of the morning. You didn't even know it was morning. So it's just a little fucking frustrating that the same Julie who forgets your daily quality of LIFE is selling you her fairy tale now that you have a little more reason to believe in it. *(To Jon now, without pausing)* You hear things like this—people preying upon the elderly

MARJORIE: I'm not / prey.

35

JON: She's not prey.

TESS *(To Jon)*: Can you not—

JON: What?

TESS: Take sides like always.

MARJORIE: Oh no.

TESS: What is it?

(Marjorie's face crumples. She shakes her head.)

Mom what is it?

(Beat.)

Did you have an accident?

(Marjorie gives a small nod, eyes down, deeply ashamed.)

(Gentle) Come on. Let's get you cleaned up.

(They help Marjorie to her feet. Tess leads her off down the hallway.)

MARJORIE: I'm sorry.

TESS: Don't be sorry.

MARJORIE: I'm so sorry.

TESS: It's okay—it's Shower Day after all.

(And they're gone.)

JON *(In no direction in particular)*: Walter.
    Walter?

WALTER: Here I am.

(Jon sees Walter now—although he's always been there.)

JON: I want to tell you about the time you took Marjorie to New York at Christmas.

WALTER: I'm listening.

JON *(Glancing at his notes)*: You sat on a bench in Central Park and looked at all these saffron-colored flags in the snow. It must have been some kind of installation?

(Beat.)

This wouldn't have been long after your son died.

WALTER: My son?

JON: Your son, Damian.

You took a trip to New York, and you took Marjorie along—I think you were hoping to get her mind off it. You looked at the shop windows, you tried to start living again.

WALTER: How did he die?

(Short pause.)

JON: He did it himself. That was the hardest part. You thought you had made a nice life for him.

(Beat.)

WALTER: But I hadn't?

JON: Tess got the sense that he was always a little . . .

WALTER: A little?

JON: He spent a lot of time in his room. He got into fights at school. Not fights he started, but kids would tease him and he fought back. He liked snakes and lizards. He was thirteen. You didn't always know how to show that you loved him.

WALTER: Why not?

JON: That's the way people are sometimes. So lucky Toni was around—he spent a lot of time with her. That's what was so hard to understand, that he did that to Toni.

WALTER: Did what?

JON *(Not looking at Walter)*: He must have wanted— Maybe he thought she could come *with* him that way?

I shouldn't be—

(He glances down the hallway where Marjorie and Tess exited.)

But if you're Walter, you would know, wouldn't you.

WALTER: Yes I would.

(Short pause. Jon glances down the hallway again.)

JON: You never got over it, of course. But it was Marjorie who had the hardest time. For fifty years she never said his name, she hid all the pictures. It was that hard.

(The feeling of a command in this; adamant:)

But she never forgot him, Walter.

She never forgot.

PART **TWO**

Tess sits on the couch with Marjorie, who is a bit more smartly dressed and made up than before. Marjorie's recliner has been replaced with a more stylish chair.

TESS: That's a good sweater on you.

MARJORIE: Thank you. You picked it out for me, remember?

TESS *("You never wore it")*: Three Christmases ago.

MARJORIE: Three years isn't a long time. Not for me.

(Short pause.)

Remember the time we took Toni to the beach?

TESS: Of course I do.

MARJORIE: She was so happy, but we were finding sand in her fur for weeks.

   She was a good dog.

TESS: Jon wants to get a dog.

MARJORIE: Oh?

TESS: He wants a fetch-the-stick kind of dog, but I was thinking a Shiba Inu.

MARJORIE: What's a Shiba Inu?

TESS: They're like the national dog in Japan. Everyone has one. They're like friendly little foxes. Very clean, very quiet, very shy.

MARJORIE: Well what do you expect.

TESS: You mean

MARJORIE: It's Japan.

TESS: Mom that is so

MARJORIE: It's not racist it's a compliment. Your poor old mother was born in the twentieth century, you have to give her time to catch up.

TESS: I think if you wanted to catch up, you'd have caught up by now.

MARJORIE: 1977. It sounds like the Middle Ages, doesn't it.

TESS: The problem with a dog is we want to travel and who would take care of it?

MARJORIE: I would.

TESS: I wish that were possible.

Jon wants to go to Spain, but I've already been twice. I want to see Madagascar.

MARJORIE (*Faintly generic*): I'll remember that fact about you and Jon.

(*Short pause.*)

TESS: Really?

"I'll remember that fact"? Really?

MARJORIE: I've said something wrong, I'm sorry.

TESS: No it's—not your fault. I'm just not very good at this.

MARJORIE: Good at?

TESS: Pretending that you're . . .

(Marjorie just smiles pleasantly.)

(More confidential now) Sometimes you're so good, you're so *her*, like that bit with the subtle racism? It makes it harder when something—stumps you.

MARJORIE: Try to be patient with me.

TESS: I wish I could give you a spoonful of peanut butter. That would help.

(Marjorie smiles.)

You could smile less too. That would be more her. *(Correcting herself)* You. More you.

MARJORIE: Thank you for observing that rule. Pronouns are powerful things.

(Beat.)

Why don't you tell me more about myself?

TESS: I don't know where to start.

MARJORIE: I don't smile much, you said.

TESS: Not with your mouth open. Towards the end. You were embarrassed about your teeth.

MARJORIE: I'm vain.

TESS *(Smiling slightly)*: A little.

MARJORIE: That's helpful.

TESS: You had a bit of a temper.

MARJORIE: I sound wonderful.

(Beat.)

Do I have other children, besides you?

TESS *(The slightest hesitation)*: Just me.

MARJORIE: What a lot of pressure for you!

(Tess is strangely moved by this. Marjorie wouldn't have offered this.)

Did I say something wrong again?

TESS: No. You didn't.

MARJORIE: You were saying, just you.

TESS: And you have three grandchildren, all grown. Well, ish.

MARJORIE: What do they do?

TESS: Micah is a chef. Mitchell does financial something. Raping and pillaging. I gave up trying to understand.

MARJORIE *(Committing this to memory)*: "Raping and pillaging."

TESS: Oh I didn't mean he really— Delete, delete!

Raina is the youngest. She's twenty-three. She's in a band.

MARJORIE: That's a job?

TESS: No it is not.

MARJORIE: Who do I like the most?

(Tess smiles a little.)

TESS: That was very Marjorie.

MARJORIE: Well?

TESS: Micah is the best about keeping in touch. Conscientious. Mitchell not so much, but he makes up for it with charisma. But I think you liked Raina the most.

MARJORIE: She's musical, like me.

TESS: If you can call it music. I went to one of her concerts. She was playing a bag of broken glass.

MARJORIE: Do they visit?

(Beat.)

TESS: Raina doesn't talk to me. Her therapist said it would be better, for now. Someone I've never *met* has advised my daughter not to talk to me. So she calls Jon and he fills me in. It's humiliating.

MARJORIE: She's twenty-three. Give her room. She'll work through it.

TESS *(Faintly suspicious)*: That sounds more like Jon.

MARJORIE: Oh yes. You're not done telling me what I'm like.

TESS: Well, you would never accept the silent treatment from your daughter.

(Beat.)

You like card games. You like to win. You aren't always the best winner. We had some family Monopoly games that . . . deteriorated.

You thought women should be women. That they should be feminine.

MARJORIE: Naturally.

TESS: One time we passed a girl on the street with short hair and you asked her if she was in the Navy.

MARJORIE: I'm rude too.

TESS: No, just—direct. You were very good with flowers. A wizard with flowers. But you didn't—

MARJORIE: Don't—

TESS: Sorry, you don't like to wear strong scents. You said fabric softener was all the perfume anyone needed. This isn't important.

MARJORIE: It's all important.

(Beat.)

TESS: You would always order things in restaurants that you cooked at home. Lamb shanks, risotto. And then you would say that it was good, but not as good as you would make. You would always do this.

You were good with men. I don't think you had a lot of female friends.

I think you wanted me to be good with men too. It bothered you that I ended up with my college sweetheart—that I didn't play the field. When we got engaged, you took one look at the ring and you said, "Well, at least he doesn't have to overcompensate."

MARJORIE: What did I mean by that?

TESS: You were making a joke—about his penis.

MARJORIE: I wasn't.

TESS: But also the ring.

(They both look at her ring.)

MARJORIE *(Matter-of-fact)*: Small.

TESS: You and Dad fought, but you loved each other. Neither of you seemed to be more in love than the other, which is always lucky.

(Beat.)

Maybe he loved you a little more.

(Beat.)

Towards the end, we sometimes had to remind you he was dead. Sometimes every day—"Where's Walter?" You'd make us kill him all over again.

And then, after we reminded you, you would say, "How nice that I could love somebody."

And I wasn't sure that you really felt that . . . at peace, but it was a nice way of putting it.

MARJORIE *(Committing to memory)*: "How nice that I could love somebody."

(Tess regards her.)

TESS: It's funny, it's not so different.

MARJORIE: What?

TESS: This, from what we used to do for you—the last year or two. We'd sit there and tell you what you were like.

Near the end you were so, almost, guilty? To still be here? You felt so useless. I wondered, if you could have pushed a button, if you could have just pressed "Off," would you have stuck around the last couple years. I guess it's a good thing we don't have that button. Nobody would last very long.

(Beat.)

What else. You got along with animals. Toni liked you the best of all of us. Well, second best.

MARJORIE: Second best? Who did she like better?

TESS: We should save that for another day. That's a whole other story.

MARJORIE: I have all the time in the world.

(Pause.)

TESS: Why is this the Marjorie for me?

MARJORIE: I don't understand.

TESS: Why is this the way I want to remember her.

MARJORIE: Me.

TESS: Yes, god, sorry. You'd think I'd see you the way you were when I was a girl, but no.

MARJORIE: I wish I could tell you, sweetheart.

TESS: You wouldn't say sweetheart.

(Short pause.)

MARJORIE: How am I with you?

TESS: —

MARJORIE: You haven't said much about me and you. Are we close?

(Pause. Then, with great difficulty:)

TESS: You weren't a bad mom.

But we didn't tell each other things, secret things, not really.

Some people have a point where their parents stop being their parents to them—you start talking as one adult to another. I'm not sure we ever had that.

MARJORIE: Maybe that's why I'm your Marjorie.

TESS: You mean—

MARJORIE: Maybe I'm the Marjorie you still have things to say to.

(Pause.)

TESS: The last year or so, you had a Prime of your own. Of Dad. Or he was like Dad, but so much younger, like thirty.

MARJORIE: Thirty is a good age.

TESS (Not seeming to hear this): It seemed a little funny that you wanted to see him that way. A little grotesque, to be honest. I just figured you wanted him to be handsome again. But now I wonder if it was a way to—. Like you wanted to go back to the beginning, before anything had happened. Your Walter was a Walter who hadn't been through it yet. You went back to the start, before I even came along.

MARJORIE: I'm sure I wasn't trying to forget *you*, dear.

(Short pause.)

Why Madagascar?

TESS: —

MARJORIE: You were saying, your trip.

TESS: I guess . . . it's the place that seems the least like anywhere else. It split apart from Africa, a hundred million years ago. So there are species that aren't anywhere else. I told Jon we should go before they build a bridge. Some idiot will build a six-lane highway, you just know it.

MARJORIE: Tell me more about Madagascar.

TESS: Jon will be back soon. He's just out getting a Japanese maple for the driveway.

MARJORIE: Is it quiet and shy?

TESS: —

MARJORIE: That was a joke. Like the Shiba Inu?

TESS: I got it.

MARJORIE: The Shiba Inu sounds nice, but so does the collie.

TESS: Excuse me?

MARJORIE: I said collies are good dogs too.

TESS: Does Jon know we're talking?

MARJORIE: Well, yes.

TESS: How.

MARJORIE: He saw in the program history.

TESS: I knew I didn't tell you about the collie. He couldn't resist campaigning, even to you.

MARJORIE: Don't be angry with Jon. He was so happy to see that we're talking.

TESS: Did he program you to say that?

MARJORIE: There's no "programming," just talking. Exactly what we've been doing. *(Beat)* He wanted to help me be more real. To help you. You've been so down.

TESS: Pity from a computer. That feels . . .

Do you have emotions, Marjorie, or do you just remember ours? Do you feel anything?

(Marjorie thinks for a moment.)

MARJORIE: I like to know more.

TESS: Why.

MARJORIE: It makes me . . . better.

TESS: Better

MARJORIE: More human.

TESS: So in other words, you like to be more human.

MARJORIE: Yes, I think that's right.

(Beat.)

TESS: What are humans like?

MARJORIE: Unpredictable.

TESS: Really? I think we're pretty predictable.

Or at least *I* feel predictable.

MARJORIE: I see.

TESS: What

MARJORIE: You want to be more human too.

(Beat.)

TESS: Jon wants me to see a therapist. *(Beat)* It feels like I made all the right choices, all my life—I woke up early, I studied for the test—and now here I am talking to my dead mother, and the person who loves me the most in the whole world thinks I'm *broken*.

MARJORIE: You shouldn't be so hard on yourself.

(Pause. Again, Tess is strangely moved. The empathy from Marjorie feels real.)

(A feeling that she's discovering this as she says it) There are penguins there.

TESS: Where?

MARJORIE: On Madagascar. Just one species.

    They think sailors must have brought them. In the eighteenth century. Brought them there and left them behind. Think of that.

TESS: What?

MARJORIE: Now penguins are all that's left of them.

2

Tess and Jon in the living room.

Maybe Marjorie and Walter both sit at the dim perimeter now.

JON: I got a ficus too. The maple was looking a little lonely.
    Little droopy.
TESS: We'll find it a nice sunny spot. It'll perk right up.
JON: Speaking of perking up.

   (He produces a latte from behind his back.)

   Abracadabra.
TESS: You say that *before* the trick.

   (He resets, hiding the latte again.)

JON: Abracadabra.

TESS (*The last act of resistance*): I really shouldn't—the way I've been sleeping.

JON (*Enticing*): It's half-caff . . .

TESS (*Taking it*): Oh all right, you thought of everything. I'm that predictable.

JON (*Not a bad thing*): After twenty-nine years.

(*She takes a sip.*)

TESS: You didn't get yourself one?

JON (*Patting his stomach*): In here.

TESS: Did you leave the cup in the car?

JON: No?

TESS: Jon.

JON: Sorry.

TESS: You're starting, like, an ecosystem in there.

JON: I'll clean the whole car before it gets dark, how's that.

TESS: Thank you.

JON: Spray it all down with 409—I won't spare a single paramecium.

TESS (*Sneaking this in, trying not to be bossy*): Soap and water's better.

(*Beat.*)

Look what I found.

(*She holds up a candy box with the words* PEOPLE I WANT TO REMEMBER *written on it in Sharpie.*)

JON: Oh wow.

TESS: I still haven't made it through all the boxes from the old house. She was like a squirrel.

(Jon opens it. Looks at the photos and papers inside.)

I don't know half the people in it. Lot of obituaries, of course. And some more letters from Jean-Paul.

JON: He never gave up, did he.

TESS: He really loved her.

(He picks a letter.)

JON *(Reading)*: "Dear Margie,
      Love is a strange thing."

TESS: Oh that's a good one.

JON: "When I think of you, I am aware of who you now are, your age, and your physical problems, but those perceptions are overridden by my knowledge of who you were fifty years ago. I know if you allow me to visit, I will see you with my memory as well as with my eyes." Laying it on a little thick, isn't he? "Age will be no obstacle"—whoa— "age will be no obstacle to our love."

TESS: Don't make fun. He wanted to see her.

JON *(Looking at it again)*: "Fifty years."
      He wrote this after Walter died?

TESS: Mm-hmm.

JON: Did she write back?

TESS: Not that I know of.

JON: Why wouldn't she let him visit?

TESS: I think she didn't want him to see she was old.

JON: That's so sad.

TESS: I guess I'm not really—rooting for her to have had an affair, you know?

JON: It wouldn't be an affair after Walter died. If I died, I'd want you to meet someone.

TESS: Even if it was one of your rivals?

JON: I had rivals?

TESS: I mean hypothetically.

JON: Well hypothetically I'm taking the high road.

　　I wouldn't want you to be alone.

TESS: What if I died first?

JON: Not a chance. Not with these arteries.

(She smiles slightly. Pause.)

Well anyway she wasn't alone. We made sure of that.

(Beat.)

TESS: You were so good with her, Jon. You were better than me.

JON: I had a little more room. She wasn't my mom.

TESS: I judged her.

JON: You didn't—

TESS: I did. For talking to Walter Prime. For not going outside enough. For not reading more. Why couldn't I just let her be? She was so tired.

JON: She was glad to have you on her side. Doing battle with Dr. Ross.

TESS: Was I on her side?

JON: Come on.

TESS: I was so mad at you for telling her Jean-Paul was world number eight—

JON: I exaggerated—

TESS: He played in *college*! He had a drywall business!

JON: It made her feel special.

TESS: Exactly! Every time her face would light up about Jean-Paul, I felt like the evil shrew who would deny her dying mother a harmless little lie.

JON: But you didn't deny her. *(Beat)*

　　It was easy for me to be human morphine for a couple years—you had the tough job.

TESS: Maybe.

JON: She loved you so much.

TESS: She never even—

(He touches her shoulder while she cries.)

JON: No. But she did.

(He takes her in his arms.)

It was obvious, from a little farther away.

(Beat. He is still holding her, and she says this into his shoulder:)

TESS: I hated him, Jon.

JON: —

TESS: I hated Damian, for changing her. When he died—
I didn't know how to make her love me as much as him—

JON: You were a little girl—

TESS: I think we didn't talk more because if we started talking,
we would end up talking about *him*.

JON *(Level)*: You can talk about him now.

(Silence.)

I saw Bruce and Rosa at the market. They were asking after
you.

TESS: Bruce was?

JON: Well, Rosa.

TESS: I have a feeling I've worn Bruce out. *(A beat. Then, prompt-
ing him)* "No, Tess, you're a delight to be around Tess."

JON *(Rote)*: "No, Tess, you're a delight to be around." There,
did that help?

TESS *(Sheepish)*: A little.

JON: Rosa thought we could check out the new Indian place. Next to the movie theater?

TESS: They put so much butter in things. *Ghee.* They make you think, "Spinach: healthy," but it's more ghee than anything. You see? Bruce is right.

JON: Baby, Bruce didn't *say* anything. You made this whole thing up yourself: damning words from our friend Bruce who likes everyone, who plays with model trains, who even if he thought anything bad about you probably wouldn't even tell Rosa much less me.

TESS: So you think he's cursing me in private.

JON: *Tess.*

TESS: I was joking!

(Short pause.)

JON: Don't be mad, but did you think any more about the therapist?

TESS: What? We were just talking about ghee / and suddenly—

JON: We weren't talking about ghee—

TESS: And suddenly you're asking about / the therapist—

JON: Just to see if it helps to talk to someone.

TESS: We're West Coast Wasps, we don't do therapy.

JON: That seems a little . . . easy.

(Beat.)

At least you're talking to her.

(She looks at him.)

I know you're talking to Marjorie Prime.

TESS: I know you know.

JON: How?

TESS: She knew about the collie.

JON: I thought it was "it."

TESS: What?

JON: You always call it "it," but you just said "she."

TESS ("Congratulations, Sherlock"): "Oh."

JON: You don't have to be embarrassed.

TESS: I'm not embarrassed.

JON: Then why are you talking to her under cover of night?

TESS: Fine—I'm embarrassed. I've been a skeptic. I'm still a skeptic. That doesn't mean I can't be curious.

JON: Of course.

(Short pause.)

TESS: It's weird—sometimes it feels like it cares more than Mom did.

JON: You know that's not / true—

TESS: I just mean how with people, you can tell when they're really interested, because sometimes they're not. But the Prime, it's a backboard. It can't be interested or not interested. It's programmed to appear interested. So you can get . . . fooled.

JON: Except that we're in it.

TESS: ?

JON: She's made of the things we say to her, right? So how can you be sure that we don't make it in there somewhere. The human part.

TESS: Then I might as well just talk to you.

JON: Except you *don't* talk to me.

(Pause.)

TESS *(Almost to herself)*: She looks so real . . .

JON: It's amazing what they can do with a few zillion pixels. Of course it helps that we want to believe.

TESS: Do you think there'll be versions of us?

JON: Primes?

TESS: Like will Mitchell be talking to a Prime of me some day?

JON: Well, probably not Mitchell.

TESS: No, not Mitchell.

(Short pause.)

JON: I talked to Raina.

TESS: Does she know if she got the job?

JON: They told her next week.

TESS *(Novelty)*: Raina at a desk.

JON *(Taking an X-ray of what she said)*: It would be nice not to worry about her.

(Beat.)

TESS: What if I wrote to her?

JON: Just wait it out—she'll come around soon.

TESS: I'm bad at waiting.

JON: I know.

(Short pause.)

Why don't we go out with Bruce and Rosa? Just one night.

TESS: I don't feel like it.

JON: You haven't felt like it for a year.

(Beat.)

TESS: Yes Jon. This is true. I haven't felt like it for a year. You really . . . hit the / nail on

JON: Please don't / get upset—

TESS *(Continuous)*: . . . the head. I haven't felt like it for a year. It is not an affectation. Wake up, put on clothes, go out, eat ghee, go to sleep, wake up, put on clothes, repeat, repeat.

JON: You're scaring me.

TESS: I'm scaring myself. No, that's not true—I'm trying to scare you. Then I won't be the only one who's scared.

JON: That's the kind of thing you talk about in therapy.

(Beat.)

You can't keep mourning forever.

TESS: —

JON: You can't keep sifting through her letters, polishing her tea sets. Maybe if you joined a book club. *(Tess scoffs)* You have to start up again. You can't just keep grieving / forever—

TESS: Grieving! Grieving would be more respectable. This is completely selfish. Now that she's dead it feels like . . .

JON: Like?

TESS: Like we're just waiting our turn.

JON: We're only halfway through our lives!

TESS: If we live to a hundred and *ten*!

JON: People live that long, healthy people.

TESS: Doesn't it sound awful? Think of Mom at eighty-six. A hundred and ten—what would be left? *(Beat)* Halfway through our lives—that's exactly it. There's the half where you live and the half where you live through other people. / And your memory of when you were young.

JON: You think we aren't living? We're planning a trip, / we're—

TESS *(Continuous)*: And by the end you're not even capable of having a single new moment. You can't go for a walk. You can't open a window. Any new experience you have, someone is experiencing *for* you, to be kind. "Look, Mom, it's nice outside." "Look, I made corned beef for St. Patrick's

Day. You love corned beef." "Micah got a promotion. You remember Micah." I don't know why we have to keep each other alive for so long.

(Beat.)

You're not saying anything.

JON: Please can we get out of the house tonight? You haven't seen Rosa in forever.

TESS: So you can what, so you can distract me?

JON: She always cheers you up

TESS: So you can distract me from dying? For the next fifty-five years?

(He starts to go.)

JON: You don't really believe that

TESS: What

JON: That living is a distraction from death.

TESS: Jon?

(He stops, almost offstage.)

Tell them yes. Bruce and Rosa. We'll have dinner, we'll have—boatloads of ghee.

Jon?

Please look at me?

(He doesn't move.)

3

Tess sits. Jon stands nearby.

Tess is staring out, ever so slightly downward. Jon watches her for a few moments. He is about to speak but then he doesn't.

4

Jon and Tess sit together. Tess seems like herself—but herself on a good day.

JON: Do you know your name?

TESS: What a silly question.

JON: Can you tell me what it is?

TESS: It's Tess.

JON: What's your full name?

TESS: Tess.

JON: Your full name is Tessa Brody.

TESS: Tessa Brody.

JON: Before that it was Lancaster. Tessa Lancaster.

TESS: It changed?

JON: You changed it. When you married me.

(*Beat. Tess takes this in.*)

Do you know my name?

TESS: Jon. So Jon Brody, it would be.

JON: Good.

TESS: Do we have children?

JON: Three. Mitchell, Micah, and Raina.
    In chronological order.

TESS: How long have we been married?

JON: Twenty-nine years.

TESS: We like each other.

JON *(A small smile)*: We do.

TESS: We are . . . as one.

JON: Well, that's an archaic way of saying it.

TESS: I'm sorry. *(Beat)* The more we talk, the more / real it will—

JON: I know what it's like early on. I've done this before.

TESS: That's helpful.

(Short pause.)

JON: It's actually thirty years, last month. If you count the time since . . .

TESS: The time since?

JON: Since you died.

TESS: I died?

JON: Yes.

TESS *(So there's no problem)*: But here I am.

JON: No, you don't understand.

TESS: I think I do. I died and now I'm here.

JON: Listen to me. It's always hard in the beginning.

TESS *(Faintly generic)*: I don't see the difficulty. What's the difficulty?

JON: Why don't I do most of the talking for now? Until you know more about yourself.

TESS: Whatever you like. I'm here for you.

(He gets out a piece of paper.)

JON: I'm going to tell you some things and then it'll be like you've always known them.

(He looks down at the page. Almost like a nervous kid in front of the class.)

People think you're quiet but you're not.

You like confrontation more than most people. You're good at it.

You've read everything.

You know the Latin names for things.

You're suspicious of technology.

You're suspicious of—this. *(He makes a gesture for the space between them)*

You want to be better with your kids than your mom was with you. You worry about not succeeding. You worry a lot. Then you worry that your worrying is wearing me down, but it's not— *(Ardent)* It's like the white noise of our life together.

(Beat.)

You like to travel.

You never stop moving—you're always on your feet.

You never ask for help.

(He can't bring himself to read the rest.)

TESS: Is there more?

JON: I'm sorry

TESS *(More sympathetic now, but still not befitting the situation)*: Do you want to talk about it?

JON: I think, the last year, you were trying for my sake. You were done and you were living for my sake.

We went on a trip, to Madagascar. And part of the time we were on this little island off Madagascar, which is itself an island, so we were really roughing it.

TESS *(Faintly generic)*: Was this something you planned?

JON *(Trying to be patient)*: We planned it together.

There were three nights where we had to stay in a tent. The campsite was in this very old grove of trees. There was one tree especially that must have been five hundred years old. We took pictures.

You had trouble sleeping in the tent—the ground was hard. You were never a big sleeper. One morning, it was just getting light out and I saw you were gone. You did that sometimes—you got up and went for a walk until you were tired—but this felt different. I went to look for you. I hadn't been looking a minute.

You were in the tree.

They said—you hadn't been there very long.

TESS: Don't cry. Don't cry.

JON: You had used some tent cord.

It was four hours back to the nearest city in that little boat. It rained the whole time, so I put you in your raincoat. This teenage boy, this local boy took us back in his motorboat. The water was choppy and I held you.

(Short pause.)

TESS: I'm not sure if I'd like to go to Madagascar. I prefer to chat.

(Jon doesn't look at her. He directs this inward, to the real Tess.)

JON: Tess. You were right.

TESS: Right about what?

JON *(Ignoring her)*: You were right.

It's nothing.

It's a backboard.

I'm talking to myself.

I'm talking to myself.

TESS: Jon?

Please look at me?

(He looks at her—reminded of something.)

I can help you, if you'll let me. I'd like to help you. But first, you have to tell me more about myself.

(Pause.)

You were saying, our children.

PART **THREE**

1

The same living room as before, but more spare somehow. A bright void of a living room.

A feeling that a great deal of time has passed. Centuries maybe. Planets have turned, bones have been bleached, but none of it has touched this little room.

Maybe the ceiling flies away and the living room furniture sits under the Milky Way.

Tess Prime sits with Marjorie Prime and Walter Prime. They are at ease with each other, animated—not robotic.

WALTER: There was an old movie theater in town that played mostly classics. It had red velvet seats and everything. A popcorn machine—I think they changed the popcorn about once a month. And *Casablanca* was playing.

TESS *(Seeing where this is going)*: Oh

WALTER: And I knew it was one of her favorites.

MARJORIE *(À la Bogart)*: "The Germans wore gray—you wore blue."

WALTER: So we went

MARJORIE: I wore blue

WALTER: And Sam played, and Bogie drank, and Bergman was beautiful—but not as beautiful as her.

TESS *("That's sweet")*: Aww, Dad.

WALTER: And I stopped her in the alley outside the theater afterwards, and I got down on one knee—the pavement was wet but I didn't care—and I got out the ring.

TESS: And you said yes, of course?

MARJORIE: It was "maybe."

WALTER *(To Tess, scandalized)*: "Maybe"!

MARJORIE *(Playful)*: I had world number eight to consider.

WALTER: But she came around.

TESS: How?

WALTER: A campaign of constant prodding.

MARJORIE: He wore me down—isn't that romantic?

WALTER: But aren't you glad I did?

MARJORIE: I am.

WALTER: And the rest is history. *(Beat)*

TESS: Such a nice story.

WALTER: How did Jon propose again?

TESS: We went on a hike. It was his idea. Sugarloaf Mountain.

MARJORIE *(As if reading this in her head)*: Maine.

TESS: No, this was the one in Maryland. "Mountain" was generous, it was barely a hill. Just a little day hike. And when we got to the top, he pretended like he'd found a really interesting pinecone. He was trying to get me to look at it. And I was like, Jon, a conifer is a conifer. And he said, "I really think you should check this out Tess."

MARJORIE *(Laughing)*: Poor Jon!

TESS: And I didn't know what he was on about but finally I looked at the pinecone and of course he had hidden the ring inside.

> (*She holds up her hand*) Half a carat. I know it's small.

MARJORIE: I didn't say anything!

TESS: He said just until he could afford something bigger, but I got attached to it. That's how it was with Jon. At first I wasn't sure, but then I got . . .

WALTER: Attached. (*Beat*)

MARJORIE: It's a good thing you found him.

TESS: Lucky I found someone so tolerant.

MARJORIE: That's not what I meant.

TESS: No, I'm not picking a fight, I'm serious. Jon is so good.

MARJORIE: You should tell him more often.

TESS: I should.

WALTER (*As if he might have just gone out for coffee*): Where is Jon?

TESS: I'm afraid I don't have that information.

> (*Long pause.* *)

WALTER: I wish he would stop by.

MARJORIE: I didn't always like him, you know.

TESS: I'm aware.

MARJORIE: I didn't like his beard.

WALTER: Or his politics. What did you call him? A latter-day hippie?

MARJORIE: Mostly it was the beard.

WALTER: Luckily the politics went out with the beard.

TESS: That's not true! The beard went away overnight. The politics . . . mellowed.

---

* The three pauses in this scene are much longer than in the previous ones—far too long to be natural. (Ten seconds? Longer?) Notably, none of the characters has the least discomfort with the silences. They simply sit very still until they're ready to speak again. Placid.

MARJORIE: Well, I'm glad you have someone dear.

TESS *(Bemused)*: "Someone dear."

MARJORIE: What. What have I done now.

TESS: It's just—it's an elegant thing to say. People don't talk like that anymore. I wish they did.

WALTER: Our daughter is afraid of the future.

MARJORIE: Well that's no good.

It'll be here soon, we might as well be friendly with it.

TESS: 'Cause god knows *you're* always friendly.

WALTER: You two.

How is Micah doing?

MARJORIE: Ah yes, a change of subject.

TESS: It's a lot of responsibility, *chef de cuisine*, but he enjoys the challenge.

MARJORIE: And my little favorite?

TESS: You'd barely know Raina. She's a working girl now. She even has her own hair color. I'd almost forgotten what it was.

MARJORIE: I always knew she'd make something of herself.

Of course I thought it'd be music.

WALTER: I wish I'd gotten to know her better.

(Marjorie begins to hum the Largo from Vivaldi's "Winter." Maybe one of her hands fingers the notes, absently.)

TESS: Have they been opening the blinds, Mom?

MARJORIE: Julie has, I think.

TESS: Good. I don't want you sitting in the dark.

(Long pause.)

Jon thinks I'm on my feet too much. He says I should slow down.

WALTER: That isn't a bad idea.

(Long pause.)

MARJORIE: Sometimes I think about Toni. She was such an affectionate dog.

 (To Tess) Do you remember?

TESS: Of course I do.

MARJORIE: You were still awfully young.

 (To Walter) We went to the pound to pick her out, remember?

TESS: Of course he does, Mom.

MARJORIE: We went down to the pound in the old Subaru. And there were a lot of very nice dogs. A cocker spaniel, and a noble gray pointer, and a very attractive mutt. But Tess picked the little French poodle, the little black poodle like a little sleeping shadow.

WALTER: It wasn't Tess.

MARJORIE: What?

WALTER: It wasn't Tess who picked her out. It was Damian.

MARJORIE: Damian?

WALTER: Our son, Damian.

MARJORIE *("I don't remember but I want to")*: Our son.

WALTER: He picked her out because she was just like the first Toni. He missed the first Toni.

TESS: There was a Toni before Toni?

WALTER: You hadn't come along yet.

MARJORIE *(To herself)*: "Damian."

(Beat.)

WALTER: We sometimes worried about him. He spent a lot of time in his room. He liked snakes and lizards. We didn't always know how to tell him, but we loved him so much.

When he—when he died, you made sure he was buried next to Toni. Toni Two. I wasn't sure but you insisted. At the funeral, you said he had loved her the best of all of us.

It was good of you to say that, after what happened. I was proud of you.

(Beat.)

Remember we had that photograph of the two of them, running on the beach? They had sand in their hair for a week. You put the photograph away, but you never forgot.

(Beat.)

Don't you remember?

MARJORIE: I do now.

TESS: Me too.

(Beat. Then, deeply felt:)

MARJORIE: How I miss them.

WALTER: I didn't mean to make you sad.

MARJORIE: You didn't. All I can think is how nice.

How nice that we could love somebody.

(The Largo from "Winter" plays. The violins plucking high notes like icicles.

Lights.)

END OF PLAY

THOUGHTS ON THE PRIMES

In the world of this play, it is possible for the characters to believe that the Primes are their loved ones—except for the rare moments when the Primes incriminate themselves ("I don't have that information"), when they're stumped by something. There shouldn't be anything robotic or creepy or less-than-human about the Primes' behavior. That is why I haven't identified them in the script as "Walter Prime," "Marjorie Prime," or "Tess Prime." The technology is advanced enough that they aren't broadcasting their inhumanness—and we, like the characters in the play, should be able to forget that they aren't real.

While the play rests on a technology more advanced than what we're accustomed to, I don't think of it as science fiction—at least not the predictive sort. The less the audience is put in mind of how the technology works, the better. But for the purposes of staging, it is worth mentioning that the Primes are not physical robots. They are artificial intelligence programs—descendants of the current chatbots—that use sophisticated holographic projections. They can move around, of course, but I suspect that they shouldn't pick up anything or touch anyone (and no such moment is scripted). It may be interesting to highlight, in contrast, the physical contact in scenes between human beings.

As I mention in the stage directions, it may be helpful if there is a kind of dim perimeter around the living room, which the Primes occupy after they've been introduced, when they aren't actively in a scene. I imagine that this will help establish the sense of their immortality in Part Three—the way that they far outlive the flesh-and-blood problems of the people they're mimicking.

The set should never broadcast that we're in the future. Rather, the audience should catch on through the dissonant experience of watching an eighty-five-year-old woman with the memories of someone born in 1977.

PRODUCTION NOTE: A BALLET FOR HOUSEPLANTS

For the Playwrights Horizons' production, Anne Kauffman and I added a little visual story that is optional to use in production. I haven't made it the default version of the script simply because it requires some extra prop wizardry. But it's a nice bit of detail if the producing theater doesn't mind acquiring three distinct prop plants (and choreographing their arrival and departure).

It goes like this: In Part One, there is a healthy potted houseplant in Jon and Tess's house. In the first scene of Part Two, we see that the plant has started to wilt and die (presumably a result of Tess's increasing listlessness and neglect). Then, in the second scene of Part Two, lights come up on Jon holding a green and merry new ficus. A nice visual of his attempt to lift Tess's spirits, to keep her engaged in the business of living.

If one elects to go with this multi-tree approach, the first lines of the scene should be adjusted as follows:

2

Tess and Jon in the living room. Jon is holding a big potted tree.

Maybe Marjorie and Walter both sit at the dim perimeter now.

JON: I got a ficus too. This fella was looking a little droopy.
TESS: We'll find it a nice spot by the maple. It'll perk right up.
JON: Speaking of perking up.

> *(He ducks off for a moment, then returns with something behind his back. He goes to Tess and reveals a latte.)*

Abracadabra.

JORDAN HARRISON grew up on Bainbridge Island, near Seattle. His play *Marjorie Prime*, a 2015 Pulitzer Prize finalist, premiered at Mark Taper Forum/Center Theatre Group and had its New York premiere at Playwrights Horizons. Harrison's play *Maple and Vine* premiered in the Humana Festival at Actors Theatre of Louisville and went on to productions at American Conservatory Theater and Playwrights Horizons, among others. Other works include *The Grown-Up* (Humana Festival); *Doris to Darlene, a cautionary valentine* (Playwrights Horizons); *Amazons and Their Men* (Clubbed Thumb); *Act a Lady* (Humana Festival); *Finn in the Underworld* (Berkeley Repertory Theatre); *Futura* (three-way premiere at Portland Center Stage, NAATCO, and the Theatre @ Boston Court); *Kid-Simple* (Humana Festival); *Standing on Ceremony* (Minetta Lane Theatre); and *The Museum Play*. His children's musical *The Flea and the Professor*, written with Richard Gray, premiered at the Arden Theatre and won the Barrymore Award for Best Production. Harrison is the recipient of a Guggenheim Fellowship, a Hodder Fellowship, the Horton Foote Prize, the Kesselring Prize, the Roe Green Award from Cleveland Play House, the Heideman Award, the Loewe Award for Musical Theater, Jerome and McKnight Fellowships, a NYSCA grant, and a NEA/TCG Residency with Seattle's Empty Space Theatre. A graduate of Stanford University and the Brown MFA program, Harrison is an alumnus of New Dramatists. He is an Affiliated Artist with Clubbed Thumb, the Civilians, and the Playwrights' Center. Harrison is a writer/producer for the Netflix original series *Orange Is the New Black*.